WHEN I GROW UP
I'LL BE A LIBRARIAN

BY CONNIE COLWELL MILLER

ILLUSTRATED BY SILVIA BARONCELLI

AMICUS ILLUSTRATED • AMICUS INK

For the Goergen Kids–C.C.M.

Amicus Illustrated and Amicus Ink are imprints of Amicus
P.O. Box 1329, Mankato, MN 56002
www.amicuspublishing.us

LIBRARY OF CONGRESS CATALOGING-IN-PUBLICATION DATA
Names: Miller, Connie Colwell, 1976- author. | Baroncelli, Silvia, illustrator.
Title: I'll be a librarian / by Connie Colwell Miller ; illustrated by Silvia Baroncelli.
Description: Mankato, MN : Amicus/Amicus Ink, [2019] | Series: When I grow up...
Identifiers: LCCN 2017056344 (print) | LCCN 2018024923 (ebook) | ISBN 9781681514796 (pdf) | ISBN 9781681513973 (library binding) | ISBN 9781681523170 (pbk.)
Subjects: LCSH: Library science–Vocational guidance–Juvenile literature. | Librarians--Juvenile literature.
Classification: LCC Z682.35.V62 (ebook) | LCC Z682.35.V62 M55 2019 (print) | DDC 020.23–dc23
LC record available at https://lccn.loc.gov/2017056344

EDITOR: Rebecca Glaser
DESIGNER: Kathleen Petelinsek

Printed in the United States of America

HC 10 9 8 7 6 5 4 3 2 1
PB 10 9 8 7 6 5 4 3 2

ABOUT THE AUTHOR
Connie Colwell Miller is a writer, reader, and teacher who lives in Mankato, Minnesota. When she was little she always knew she would work with two things: kids and books. Today, her dream has come true. She has written over 100 books for kids, and she lives with four wonderful, creative children of her own.

ABOUT THE ILLUSTRATOR
Silvia Baroncelli has loved to draw since she was a child. She collaborates regularly with publishers in drawing and graphic design from her home in Prato, Italy. Her best collaborators are her four nephews, daughter Ginevra, and organized husband Tommaso. Find out more about her on the web at silviabaroncelli.it

Every day after school, my brother Gabe and I run to the den. We each pick a book to read. While we choose, I pretend . . .

I'm Olivia, a real-life librarian! I'm in charge of the public library. I recommend books for patrons of all ages. I help all kinds of readers—people who love to read and people who don't.

The Little Frog

My first patron is Nadia. She is writing a report about frogs. I help her do research. I show her how to find books, magazine articles, and good sources on the Internet.

A big part of my job is helping patrons with computers. Nate wants the newest book by his favorite author. I show him how to search for books in our library catalog. Julia needs help using an online database.

Search

Our library has books, audio books, eBooks, and more! Another part of my job is to maintain the library's collection. This means that I help choose and order new materials for the library.

news of the year
CATALOG

I need to keep our materials organized. I catalog new books and materials when they come in. Then patrons can find them in the library catalog and on the shelves.

FOR SALE
FOR SALE
DAMAGED

To maintain the collection, I have to get rid of books, too. Librarians call this "weeding." I pull old, damaged, and outdated books, off the shelves. The library sells some books in a big sale. Others we donate or recycle.

I don't work alone. My assistants help shelve books and other items after they're returned. They help patrons check out books and movies. And today, Teddy needs a new library card!

THE DRAGON

My library holds events, too. Some events are for kids. I help plan story times and summer reading programs to get kids excited about books. I organize monthly book clubs.

Other events are for adults. I ask writers to come and speak to people in the community. And I organize adult book clubs and readings, too.

When I grow up, I'll be a helpful librarian. But today, I've found the perfect book to read—and one for Gabe, too!
THE DRAGON
Treasure

WORDS LIBRARIANS SHOULD KNOW

catalog—To organize in an orderly way, usually by numbers or letters.

collection—All the materials available for use in a library.

database—A set of related information that is organized and stored on a computer or online.

library catalog—A searchable listing of all the materials a library owns.

patron—A person who visits the library and uses its services.

research—The act of collecting information about a certain topic.

weeding—Getting rid of old or outdated materials in a library collection.

PRACTICE BEING A LIBRARIAN SCAVENGER HUNT

Try hunting down some things at the library so you can practice being a librarian!

WHAT YOU NEED

A few pieces of paper
Ruler
Pencil
Access to a library
A friend to play with

WHAT YOU DO

1. Use the ruler and the pencil to make five rows of five boxes each (25 total boxes) on a piece of paper.
2. In each of the boxes, jot down something your friend should hunt down in the library. Here are some things a librarian might need to find. Add your own ideas, too!

   - ☐ A chapter book in a series
   - ☐ A board book about trucks
   - ☐ A book about dolphins
   - ☐ Today's local newspaper
   - ☐ An audio book on CD
   - ☐ A cookbook for kids
   - ☐ A movie
   - ☐ A map of your state

3. When you have 25 items for your friend to find, challenge him/her to complete the scavenger hunt. Your friend should mark off each box with an X when he/she finds the book or material.
4. When your friend has found all the items, switch places so YOU can be the librarian.